AF434243

THE POWER TO GET WEALTH
By Tanya Powell-Edwards

Copyright © 2021 by Tanya Powell-Edwards
All rights reserved. No part of this book may be
reproduced in any form or by any means electronic,
mechanical, photocopying, recording, or otherwise without
the written and prior permission of the publisher.

ISBN: 978-976-96622-0-9
Publisher: Engaging Conversation
Contact: conversation@tanyapowell-edwards.com

Inner Illustration: Danel Edwards
Edited By: Shanique Shand

Unless otherwise noted, all Scriptures quoted in this Prayer Book are taken from New King James Version (NKJV)

Dedication

This book is dedicated to our Lord and Saviour Jesus Christ. It's because of his work of salvation in me that I made it to this point, where I can offer poignant advice on wealth to others. I believe that He orders my steps and I can give thanks for the darkest points of my life for they have become testimonies to strengthen others. Secondly, this book is dedicated to my mother Hyacinth Powell, a beautiful little girl from St. Elizabeth who was brought to Kingston to babysit for her older sister. She started her family early and endured hardship but instilled in her children the importance of getting an education. All her children are thankful for her strong discipline and commitment to blessing us with an education.

This book is also dedicated to my husband Ezra and our children Danel and Jeda who have seen me through a range of times and emotions. I am committed to them knowing me as a gifted mother with strong faith in God, who is always striving to learn more and do more. Most importantly, I want them to remember me as the mother who prays and strived to be obedient to God's calling on my life. Lastly, I dedicate this book to my prayer partners, those who heard my cry, comforted, prayed and stood in faith with me. All their efforts have helped to propel me into the next phase of my life, where the journey will be greater than my latter years.

Introduction

The Power to Get Wealth came from moments of prayer, first with another Christian entrepreneur and later with other friends of the faith. During a time of prayer, I sensed that God asked me whether I believed Him when he told me that he had given me power. This was a thought-provoking question and it led me to start searching for scriptures in the Bible that spoke about power. I realized that power, in its most basic definition, is really an ability to do something. This led me to share my new understanding with others while experiencing a new evolving understanding of the power to get wealth. The perspective shared is deliberately from a Biblical perspective, but the topic of wealth is also dissected by demonstrating how past failures are necessary pathways to growth and accumulating wealth God's way. You will not find a get-rich-quick scheme here, but the information will

transform your mind and prepare you spiritually and

mentally to begin a new journey to wealth and riches

God's way.

Contents

On Monday, February 8, 2021 I woke up in the morning and laid in bed praying, then I decided to go for a walk. I had internet access on my work phone, so as I walked I listened to a worship song 'Yeshua' by Jesus Image Worship for most of the time. I came home and felt so good. In the afternoon, I called my friend Jamie who is an entrepreneur and a woman of God. We do not speak often but whenever we do, it's always a blessing. We spoke that evening and eventually prayed for each other and as we did, I felt like there was a question in my spirit. It was, "*When I say I give you power, do you believe?*"

Later that evening I received an invite from my friend Robert to join a prayer line where the topic was on 'holiness'. After that Bible Study, Robert called me and we spoke at length again about the goodness of God. I think it was fair to say that my day was spent in worship. Before the end of the day, I also received a promise of money that I didn't ask anyone for. It was hard to fall asleep that night because I was so stimulated by the times of worship and prayer throughout the day.

The events further led to me calling my prayer partner Pastor Marion McCalla to share the scriptures on power with her the next day. I was delving a little deeper into the question I believed the Holy Spirit had asked me, *"When I say I give you power, do you believe?"* I went online and researched the meaning of the word 'power'. It was defined as an 'ability to do or an authority'. I got excited and thought that with Marion on the phone I can look at scriptures with the word 'power'; that was stimulating. Marion reminded me that the scripture can speak to power without the actual word being explicitly mentioned. Somehow one of the scriptures that stuck in my mind was: *"And you shall remember the Lord your God, for it is He who gives you power to get wealth, that He may establish His covenant which He swore to your fathers, as it is this day* (Deuteronomy 8:18)." Thanks to Google history, I'm able to go back and share some of the scriptures on power that I read that day with you.

For God gave a spirit not of fear but of power and love and self-control.

 (2 Timothy 1:7)

But you shall receive power when the Holy Spirit has come upon you; and you shall be witnesses to Me in Jerusalem, and in all Judea and Samaria, and to the end of the earth. (Acts 1:8)

I can do all things through Christ who strengthens me. (Philippians 4:13)

Behold I have given you authority to tread upon serpents and scorpions, and over all the power of the enemy, and nothing shall hurt you. (Luke 10:19)

For the kingdom of God is not in word but in power. (1 Corinthians 4:20)

Now to Him who is able to do exceedingly abundantly above all that we ask or think, according to the power that works in us. (Ephesians 3: 20)

And God both raised up the Lord and will also raise us up by His power. (1 Corinthians 6:14)

He gives power to the weak, And to those who have no might He increases strength. Even the youths shall faint and be weary, and the young men shall utterly fall, but those who wait on the Lord Shall renew their strength; they shall mount up with wings like eagles, they shall run and not be weary,

they shall walk and not faint. (Isaiah 40: 29 – 31)

Behold, I send the Promise of My Father upon you;

but tarry in the city of Jerusalem until you are

endued with power from on high. (Luke 24:49)

His divine power has given to us all things that

pertain to life and godliness, through the knowledge

of Him who called us by glory and virtue, (2 Peter

1:3)

For the word of God is living and powerful, and

sharper than any two-edged sword, piercing even to

the division of soul and spirit, and of joints and

marrow, and is a discerner of the thoughts and

intents of the heart. (Hebrews 4:12)

Fear not, for I am with you; be not dismayed, for I am your God. I will strengthen you, Yes, I will help you, I will uphold you with my righteous right hand. (Isaiah 41:10)

Death and life are in the power of the tongue, and those who love it will eat its fruit. (Proverbs 18:21) Therefore, confess your sins to one another and pray for one another, that you may be healed. The prayer of a righteous person has great power as it is working. (James 5:16, ESV)

Your word is a lamp to my feet and a light to my path. (Psalm 119:105)

God has spoken once, twice I have heard this: That power belongs to God. (Psalm 62:11)

But the Lord stood with me and strengthened me,

so that the message might be preached fully

through me, and that all the Gentiles might hear.

And I was delivered out of the mouth of the lion.

(2 Timothy 4:17)

Finally, my brethren, be strong in the Lord and in

the power of His might.

(Ephesian 6:10).

Praying always with all prayer and supplication in

the Spirit, being watchful to this end with all

perseverance and supplication for all the saints.

(Ephesians 6: 18)

Therefore, when Pilate heard that saying, he was the more afraid, and went again into the Praetorium, and said to Jesus, "Where are you from?" But Jesus gave him no answer. Then Pilate said to Him, "Are You not speaking to me? Do you not know that I have power to crucify you, and power to release you?" Jesus answered, "You could have no power at all against me unless it had been given you from above. Therefore the one who delivered me to you has the greater sin." (St. John 19: 8 – 11).

Behold, I stand at the door and knock. If anyone hears my voice and opens the door, I will come in to him and dine with him, and he with me.

(Revelation 3:20)

In communicating the central message of this book, I'd like to write it three different ways:

1. The power to get wealth is only one dimension of power that God has given to us.

2. The ability to get wealth is only one ability that God has given us.

3. The authority to get wealth is only one dimension of authority that God has given us.

So the ability, power, authority that God has given to us all equips us to build wealth.

My primary caregivers, my mother and father who raised me, had only elementary school education. As the family grew to include four other children, the need for provisions also grew. They took on a number of jobs in the ensuing years to earn, including gardening, sewing, selling

on construction sites, the road way and at the cinemas.
They, and more particularly my mother, were insistent that
their children will have an education as they strongly
believed that education was the way out of poverty.

As I developed into a young woman, I had some
early successes, but the inner secret of being sexually
abused by my Sunday School teacher and deacon of the
Revival Church my mother and I attended dimmed much
of my inner light. Yet, amid my frustration with myself,
family economic situation, community and my
interpretation of the world system, I harboured a deep
feeling that I was born to be wealthy. However, I was
deeply frustrated because I wasn't seeing the wealth in my
life.

I became married at the age of 22 and my husband
and I raised two children. Even though we were mostly
employed, we struggled to pay bills and provide for

ourselves and extended family. I worked in Jamaica in the areas of Media and Communication, Tertiary Education and in the Restaurant Industry. My experience as a Training Officer in the Restaurant Industry led me to accept that I was called as an entrepreneur. My life changed with that revelation.

Before I share how my life of wealth started, let me share a dream. Many years ago, I had a dream that I was in the community that I grew up in. While I was there, a lady that looked like my aunt came and said to me, *"You don't see that something is wrong with your money? You need to look after yourself."* My understanding of what she was

saying is that I need to consult a 'reader man' to get help.
In *the dream, my response to her was,* "Once upon a time I would believe you, but not anymore." Around that time, I saw a man in the dream. He was huge. He reminded me of when Jamaicans use to call people 'straptin', meaning he looked strong, and with that strength he was expected to have a loud voice like a baritone perhaps. I didn't know him. He spoke to me and I was surprised by the gentleness of his voice. When I responded to my aunt's advice to seek help for my finances, he asked me, *"What do you mean?"* I told him I was grown to believe that if you have a problem, you would seek a 'mother woman' or 'reader man' to help you understand how to deal with the problem, but I no longer believed that. I told him that when I have a problem, I pray to Jesus. The man seemed pleased. That was an important dream for me.

Wealth is important to me, but it's not by 'any means necessary'. Acquiring wealth the Biblical way is very important to me. It's such an important thing to note that in 2016 after being involved in an accident and making the decision to resign from a stressful job, was when my change came. I was on vacation in Canada when my friend called me. She told me that she was praying and the Lord gave her a word for me. She said that the Lord told her to tell me that I should stop saying that "I do not have any money." Honestly, my spirit became a little disturbed and maybe furious. I was thinking that honesty is important if I proclaim to be a Christian, and if I say I have no money that would be the truth and truth is what God loves. Yet, I had known this friend for over twenty years and I knew her to be a woman of faith and prayer. I knew she would not call me to tell me that if she didn't believe she had a word from the Lord. I struggled for a bit, unsure of what to say when I perceived myself to not have money.

Soon I begun to recognise the significance of "life and death are in the power of the tongue" and "as a man thinketh in his heart so is he". I realized that the more I declared that I have no money, the truer it became in my life. I needed to change my mind set on money and lack. Instead, I began to say, "Lord, there is space in my purse to be filled and I ask that you fill it in in Jesus' name" or "Lord, you see the amount in my account, please increase it in Jesus' name." My financial situation started changing because my mind set began to change. Here's an example of how I changed my approach:

- Once upon a time, if I owed the bank and they called me about it, I would start acting irrationally, see my situation as desperate, think of myself as a failure, wished that I

had married a rich man and cry. With my

changing mind set, I pray about my debts. If

the bank calls, I answer my phone and try to

negotiate a comfortable payment

arrangement with the agent. I apply this

principle to all debt and then strategise to

clear them.

By now you may be wondering why I was in debt,

so allow me to share. I resigned my job in late 2016

because it had gotten to the stage where when I finished

working each day, I was of no use to myself and family. I

was merely existing to work. My family did not take the

resignation well because it was my highest paying job that

came with a vehicle. Having resigned, it now meant that

the following month I did not have an income. I was also

recovering from an accident and just felt sick and weak. I had a mortgage to pay and had to start taking the bus again. At times, I wondered if I had failed but a part of me knew that I had to trust God in the season that I was in.

I was a year behind with all bills, credit card, mortgage and loan payments. I started praying about these asking God to show me the way to clear my debt. I may have asked for miracle money into my account as well, but I didn't experience that. What I did experience was a peace in prayer, less worry and an increased faith that God was going to help me somehow. I made sure to answer calls from every organization that I owed; I responsibly faced my debtors. They would often mention the times when my payments were on time and enquired what changed. I had to update them on my new financial reality.

During that time, soap-making was my hobby. I had learnt it a few years before, but didn't see myself as a business woman. I didn't want that responsibility to hire and pay others. Now that I was home and unemployed, I would sell a few soaps every now and again. I had a few soaps in a store and soon those began to sell more rapidly. Sales were increasing each week and so the store would order more. I now had to learn how to balance the needs of my home with the continuation of the business so it didn't fold. I had to accept that God had brought prophecy to pass by allowing me to be in a situation where I just had to do business in order to survive financially. It got to the point where 5 soaps were being sold each week and that increased to 10, then 15, then up to 150 and beyond. When this increase came, I started balancing paying off my loans with providing food for the home and keeping the business afloat. I managed to do all, but it was definitely not easy. The main thing that helped me in that season was the word of God in Romans 12:2 that encourages us not *be conformed to this world, but be ye transformed by the renewing of your mind, that we may prove what is good, and acceptable , and perfect will of God.* We can accomplish so much with a transformed mind.

I recall one day when the business needed to be restocked, but outstanding payments had not come in as yet because many stores who sell our products pay 30 to 45 days after receiving them. I fell out of grace with my 'transformed mind' and went into a frenzy about my lack of resources to replenish the business. My son was with me and he started ministering to me using the same things I taught him about God's Word and the peace He gives. Honestly, I was not in peace that morning. Surprisingly, at about 9:30am there was a ping on my phone and was notified that my account had been credit with over JMD $100,000.00. My son reprimanded me as I realized how I had lost my faith that morning and the deposit of the funds to the account was God's way of reminding me that before

I called on Him, He had answered. I needed to trust and He

would send the resources. I was reminded of God's

provision that day and that I do not need to expend so

much energy being afraid.

I'm sharing this story to allow you to understand

that while the acquisition of wealth is possible, it's not an

overnight affair. This is especially true for those born in

poverty. There was this time when even though I was so

cautious and thought that I did my research, I lost quarter

million Jamaican dollars. I later learnt it was a Ponzi

scheme. Years later, while reading the book of Proverbs, I

realized that wealth is like the 'coco' in the Jamaican

proverb that says, "one, one coco full basket". The basket

is not filled instantly but over a period of time. This is also

supported by scripture in Proverbs 13:11 which states,

"Dishonest money dwindles away, but whoever gathers

money little by little makes it grow." Imagine learning from the Word of God that I was destined to fail if I pursued wealth in any other way than by diligently saving, investing, following compound interest principles and not chasing high-interest-bearing accounts. This scheme contradicted the principles in the Word and that's why I was at a disadvantage and lost money.

If you're following diligently, you will remember that one of my wealth acquisition principles came from my prayer partner when she told me that I needed to stop saying that I had no money. The other principle is releasing fear in prayer, praying over your debts and knowing how you can repay so that your creditors don't lock you into an uncomfortable place. It's very important to consider the purpose of loans lest we become trapped. Proverbs 22:7 warns us that "the borrower is really a slave to the lender". It means that transitioning from debt can be quite challenging for those with numerous loans from various lending agencies. I have personally experienced the bank threatening to report me to the credit bureau to make it difficult for me to acquire loans in the future. Upon receiving the threats, I wrote to the bank thanking them for the threat and informing them of the closure of my account with them as soon as my debt was repaid in full. I have no desire to do business with an agency that threatens me, particularly when I've held an account with them for more than twenty years. Despite all the years of consistency, they chose to show little mercy when my financial situation changed

I began to wonder how public sector workers cope as from my experience, many of them acquire new loans as soon as they hear of another lending agency. Among the reasons they acquire loans are to pay rent, mortgage, school fees or buy motor vehicles. They soon find themselves struggling in debt as most of their salaries are repaying debt. This often results in them being hungry and angry on the job. Some will have other co-workers become guarantors for them so that they can borrow to consolidate their loans. If they get the consolidated loan, they will pay off the loans, but it's a matter of time before they start the debt cycle again. It can be satisfying to get borrowed money, but stressful when you have little capacity to repay. Jamaicans refer to this as "borrowing from Peter to pay Paul". It means that you have not really eliminated a debt, you have really just shifted it to another lender for the time being.

It's my hope that if you are heavily in debt but believe that you should be wealthy, that you will begin to look at wealth from a biblical perspective and begin the hard but necessary work to claw yourself from the mental and emotional stronghold of debt to begin the journey to biblical wealth. Always remember the scriptures, *"For God gave a spirit not of fear but of power and love and self-control (2 Timothy 1:7)* and *"But you shall remember the Lord your God, for it is He who is giving you power to make wealth that He may confirm His covenant which He swore to your fathers, as it is this day." (Deuteronomy 8:18)*

I'll close this section with a few more scriptures to encourage you to pray for God's wisdom and understanding. In fact, read them and later I'll help you pray a simple but impactful prayer.

But he said, "Peace be with you, do not be afraid. You're God and the God of your father has given you treasure in your sacks; I had your money." Then he brought Simeon out to them. (Genesis 43:23)

And you shall remember the Lord your God, for it
is He who gives you power to get wealth that He
may establish His covenant which He swore to your
fathers, as it is this day. (Deuteronomy 8:18)

The Lord makes poor and makes rich; He brings
low and lifts up. (1 Samuel 2:7)

Wealth and riches will be in his house, and his
righteousness endures forever.
(Psalm 112:3)

As for every man to whom God has given riches
and wealth, and given him power to eat of it, to
receive his heritage and rejoice in his labor--this is
the gift of God. (Ecclesiastes 5:19)

35

A man to whom God has given riches and wealth
and honor, so that he lacks nothing for himself of
all he desires; yet God does not give him power to
eat of it, but a foreigner consumes it. This is vanity,
and it is an evil affliction. (Ecclesiastes 6:2)

Many persons in life develop get-rich-quick

schemes that have deprived people of their hard-earned

cash. Usually, victims of these are the cash-poor and

vulnerable, many of whom have folly in their hearts about

wealth and how wealth is acquired. Perhaps, no one has

even said this to you before, especially someone saying that wealth is attainable for you. My advice to you is to stay away from get-rich-quick schemes. They rob you of your peace of mind, instead of helping you get rich. Now, I've always felt that wealth was to be mine, but I was afraid of numbers and was also very cautious with investments. However, some years ago, I heard of Cash Plus. I heard of its high returns on the funds invested and I desperately needed money. I didn't quickly get into it because I knew I was financially wise, so I asked around for advice. I asked persons in the financial sector, pastors and others, all of who gave 'good' advice. Many said that they had invested in that same company and was getting great returns. I invested JMD 250,000.00, and for two or three months, I collected $25,000.00, which was supposed to represent interest earned on the sum deposited. I felt good.

One night I went to bed and had a dream that I had
gone to the bank and could not get access to my money. In
the morning, I told my husband the dream and that I would
close my account at Cash Plus and request a cheque for the
amount invested. He suggested that he would talk to some
of his colleagues that had also invested. In the evening,
upon returning from work, he reported what his colleagues
said. They went to a meeting at Cash Plus and were told
that their investments were safe and that it's the banking
sector that was having problems because they were paying
higher interest than banks. I relaxed, thinking I understood
the dynamic of what was happening. I decided to wait a
month to see if God would speak again. He didn't, but by
the end of the month, the fund folded, and I lost all of the
amount invested. That was around 2007, and I still haven't
been compensated for a single cent of that money

(http://jamaica-gleaner.com/article/lead-stories/20160810/c

ash-plus-payout-not-investors). When these scheme

collapses, the majority of the depositors are the losers.

Over the years, I also bought into other companies

such as Avon, Amway and Herbalife. I spent money to join

some of them and some required a certain level of

investment after which you would start earning after a

certain level of expenditure or after recruitment of other

persons. I lost more than I benefited from these companies.

If you are reading this, my advice is that you should

consider carefully staying away from 'opportunities' that

ask you to pay money to join. To configure your mind,

they may invite you to meetings, usually hosted by a

charismatic trainer with a great personality.

Many times the invitations to these meetings are

from family members, friends or church members. As a

result of the trust you've developed in these persons and

the attractive amount they are earning, you may be tempted

40

to join to start earning that amount too. As soon as you pay the fee and join, they slowly start encouraging you to recommend ten to thirty persons from your phone. You make the initial contact, but they take over the conversation to do the pitching. You are even told the exact words you have to speak when presenting the company's prosperity message to others.

Once you join, you believe that you are well on your way to solving all your financial problems. You start channelling a lot of your personal finance and income into the 'opportunity' only to soon find yourself out of money and frustrated. You start resenting your friends, family and others who weren't willing to invest, or they start staying away from you because of the pressure you have placed on them. I've been there. I spent on the products, but they are so expensive that you can't keep buying because your spending power decreases. You are left to feel like a failure because you tried so hard to turn your economic situation around. The reality is that someone you don't know was becoming richer while you and your family were getting poorer.

God is a good God and is not in get-rich-quick schemes. This is why I encourage and endorse the study of wealth from the Bible's perspective because it shows wealth as power from God. In reality people have periods during which they struggle, but eventually learn over time that out of evil comes good, meaning you learn over time. Wealth is about learning to save and developing a good relationship with money where you are not constantly stressed out about what you don't have, but show appreciation for what you do have. In my opinion, wealth comes by looking at what you have and building on that over time.

If my confession and information on past financial mistakes minister to you and you have made similar mistakes, we want to repent and sin no more on this wealth journey. Below are prayers to help you get an honest conversation started with your heavenly Father about your past mistakes and seek His guidance on how to move forward.

Prayer of Repentance

Father, In Jesus' name I ask that you forgive me for my lack of understanding on matters relating to money and how I should use it to glorify you in this world. Forgive me for running after frequent loans and taking on financial stresses that you did not intend for me. Forgive me for the negative words I spoke over my life when I was frustrated. I embrace a new path with you. Please allow doors of opportunity to be opened unto me and be with me as I step into this new experience with Christ.

Father, your Word says declare that we should seek first the Kingdom of God and His righteousness and all things shall be added to us. I now ask that that you teach me to seek your Kingdom and your righteousness. Father, I acknowledge that the power to get wealth comes from you so please take the lead and teach me how to acquire wealth, how to use it wisely and how to share with others. I now ask for a new and honest wealth-generating mind-set that I can testify about. I now declare your Word upon my financial situation and look forward to abundant blessings in Jesus' name.

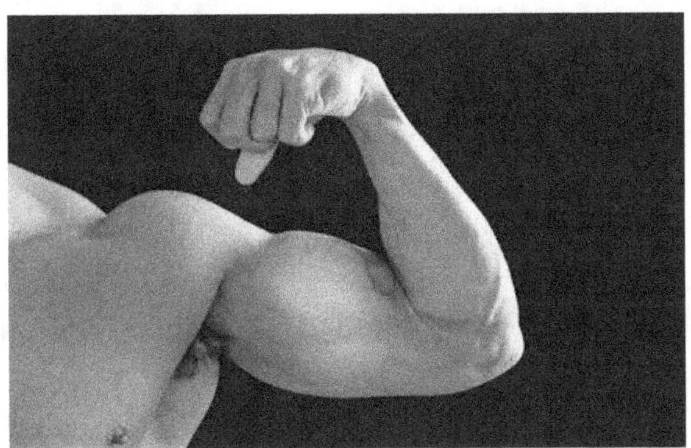

The Power to get Wealth was birthed out of what I believe was the Holy Spirit asking me this question: *"When I say I give you power, do you believe?"* This was indeed a challenging question, more so challenging for me as a Christian who is always talking about God and His work in my life. The question led me to research the meaning of the word 'power' and scriptures on 'power'. I came into the awareness that God gave us many abilities or powers, and the power to get wealth is just one of them. My focus in this season is on wealth because I've noted the significant changes over the last four years within my twenty-five or so work history.

I felt alive again and on fire as I remembered an old song and began to sing with my untrained alto voice, *"I feel like a fire shut up within my bones…"* I 'rolled back the curtains' to remember how I would feel when I felt the spirit of God moving through and upon me in my twenties through thirties.

Wealth is not a worldly concept, it is a biblical concept. The wealth of the world enslaves us while the wealth of God frees us. The wealth of the world is about taking from others and storing it while the wealth of God's kingdom is about giving and receiving. The wealth of the world is in fact stored for the righteous, but the wealth cannot be given to the righteous if they are not prepared for it because they will mismanage it. We have an example in scripture when the children of Israel were being freed from Egypt's rule and God told them to borrow gold from the Egyptians.

> *The LORD caused the Egyptians to look favourably on the Israelites, and they gave the Israelites whatever they asked for. So they stripped the Egyptians of their wealth! (Exodus 12:36)*

One could say that the Israelites got the wealth that the Egyptians had unknowingly stored for them during slavery. Later on, we see that some of the Israelites converted their wealth into idols and worshipped the idols as gods. This caused the wrath of the One that had blessed them with the wealth to erupt and the 'children' paid dearly for their improper use of the wealth given to them by God (Exodus 32). It's my reasoning that Christians should be prepared and ready to get wealth, but also to work with that wealth in a way that will keep them in right relationship with God.

I had an experience with this many years ago. I was unemployed for a while when our children were babies. After a period of time, I interviewed for a job and had an idea that it would be mine as I was given a dream about the job. The position was entry level, but the position changed to a better one even before I signed the contract. Within months, my salary became twice what it was when I started in the position and I was feeling satisfied. I worked hard and was able to help my husband take care of our children. However, around that time, my favourite aunt was spending time in Jamaica and she was making art. She gave me a bust of an African woman named *Nefertiti*. I was happy to receive the bust and took it to work. Every evening before I left work, I would put the bust in my drawer and in the mornings, I would set it on my desk. Many persons would pass by and admire it.

I was doing so well in the job, my income was increasing and I was given new responsibilities. I also had a great rapport with my supervisors, but one day I received a notice that I would be unemployed by the end of the month because economic success of the company had changed. I was devastated, but I cleared my desk and prepared for my departure from the company. I took my box home and placed the beautiful bust of Nefertiti on a piece of furniture in the living room.

Within that time period, I had a dream. I had frequent dreams, many of which manifested in reality and so, dreams were important to me. In this dream, I saw a woman in my house. She was lying in a bed in one of the bedrooms and her back was turned to me. I noticed that her hair was braided similar to that of the Egyptian women I would see in movies. At a point in the dream, I was made aware that one of the trees on the outside of the house had a snake wrapped around it. I awoke feeling unsettled about the dream and its meaning; I pondered it throughout the day. Later that day, I remembered that a guest at the place I worked had actually seen and admired the bust and had given me some information on it, but I had filed away the information without reading it. I began to search for it. When I found and read it, it told me that Nefertiti and her husband ruled in Egypt and was against God's people. I got this information years ago and so, I'll share more modern information with you below:

The earliest images of Nefertiti come from the Theban tombs of the royal butler Parennefer and the vizier Ramose, where she is shown accompanying her husband.

In the Theban temple known as Hwt-Benben ("Mansion of the Benben Stone"; the benben was a cult object associated with solar ritual), Nefertiti played a more prominent role, usurping kingly privileges in order to serve as a priest and offer to the Aton. A group of blocks recovered from Karnak (Luxor) and Hermopolis Magna (Al-Ashmunayn) shows Nefertiti participating in the ritual smiting of the female enemies of Egypt. She wears her own unique headdress—a tall, straight-edged, flat-topped blue crown.

By the end of Akhenaton's fifth regnal year, the Aton had become Egypt's dominant national god. The old state temples were closed and the court transferred to a purpose-built capital city, Akhetaton. Here Nefertiti continued to play an important religious role, worshipping alongside her husband and serving as the female element in the divine triad formed by the god Aton, the king

Akhenaton, and his queen. Her sexuality, emphasized by

her exaggeratedly feminine body shape and her fine linen

garments, and her fertility, emphasized by the constant

appearance of the six princesses, indicate that she was

considered a living fertility goddess. Nefertiti and the royal

family appeared on private devotional stelae and on the

walls of nonroyal tombs, and images of Nefertiti stood at

the four corners of her husband's sarcophagus

(https://www.britannica.com/biography/Nefertiti.

Essentially, if you are a Christian reading this, you

will see that the values of Nefertiti did not align with

Jewish faith nor with the modern day Christian faith which

outlines that there is only One God who is a jealous God

(Exodus 34: 14). It dawned on me that my sudden job loss

was due to the idolatry that I had brought into the blessing

that God had given me because light and darkness cannot

dwell in the same space. The experience was, however,

useful in that it made me aware of the spiritual world and how it can affect us in the physical realm. At the time, I revisited many of the African garments that I was wearing along with the Afrocentric jewellery and threw away or burnt some of them. When I go to buy jewellery or fabric, I pay closer attention to the symbols on them. When I make a purchase, even if there are no symbols, I still pray over them and ask God to disconnect any hidden spirits from them.

If we believe that the power or ability to get wealth is from God, we have to be in right relationship with Him. When I began to analyse whether I trusted God when He said, *"I have given you power..."* it changed many things about my life and my understanding. I began to pray again and pray differently and I began to seek first to worship God by seeking first the kingdom. I acknowledge that I had become lukewarm and lacking in fire and passion and expectation, but once I started seeking the Kingdom through acknowledging God and actively engaging in worship, I felt like I had come alive, was on fire again and receiving fresh understanding of the Word of God. My days changed and I found that I was either praying with more persons or encouraging others. I got reconnected with people I had not spoken to for years and some even called me to bless me financially even though I had not asked them for money. I also became more confident when I realised how much power God has committed to us.

The Power to get wealth is from God and it is not true wealth if it is contaminated or acquired through enslaving others. If you are unfair to others by not paying them fairly, you are storing their wealth for the day God decides to forcibly take it from you and give to the person you deprived of it.

The understanding that it is God that gives us to the power to get wealth has transformed my life. In Mark 14: 7, Jesus himself said that the poor we will always have with us, but I believe He said that because He knew that the larger majority of persons will not do the mental work to change their economic status. Didn't scripture also say that *"for we are partners working together for God, and you are God's field? You are also God's building"* (1 Corinthians 3: 9)? Co-partnership with God comes with a huge responsibility that God will not allow us to abuse.

As I close, it's important for me to note that about two weeks after being asked the question by the Lord and then exercising faith in Him because of my understanding of the Word, I heard from the Lord again. I was praying, believing God for the professional and personal requests on the vision board that I had placed before Him and praying over a 'Power to get Wealth Conference' when in my spirit came these words, *"Now that you trust me I can do wonderful things through you."* I grabbed my phone and typed it quickly. Those words assured me that God had been waiting on me to get to this point. It led me to believe that my fear and unbelief had been blocking my God-given wealth. Poverty and wealth cannot exist in the same mind because they are counterproductive to each other. Either you will serve one or the other. I acknowledge that I had difficulty believing prophecies that I had received on wealth over the years because I couldn't see enough to convince myself that these words would come to pass. My actions, my decisions, my thinking and feelings of fear was blocking the fullness of God's wealth in my life.

In closing, I recently was in conversation with a sister in Christ and shared the scripture *"For God gave a spirit not of fear but of power and love and self-control"* (2 Timothy 1:7) with her. She interjected and shared the same scripture with a graphical understanding. She expressed

that God has not given us a spirit of fear, but has given us

love, power and a sound mind. When we operate in fear,

that spirit holds *love, power and sound mind'* captive. That

is why wherever there is fear, there is no love, there is a

feeling of powerlessness and the mind is not at rest. When

you trust God, the positions are reversed whereby *love,*

power and sound mind are free to operate and fear is held

captive. My last words on the power to get wealth comes to

you from the book of Philippians 4: 4-9:

> *Rejoice in the Lord always. Again I will say,*
>
> *rejoice! Let your gentleness be known to all men.*
>
> *The Lord is at hand. Be anxious for nothing, but in*
>
> *everything by prayer and supplication, with*
>
> *thanksgiving, let your requests be made known to*
>
> *God; and the peace of God, which surpasses all*

understanding, will guard your hearts and minds through Christ Jesus.

Finally, brethren, whatever things are true, whatever things are noble, whatever things are just, whatever things are pure, whatever things are lovely, whatever things are of good report, if there is any virtue and if there is anything praiseworthy —meditate on these things. The things which you learned and received and heard and saw in me, these do, and the God of peace will be with you.

Wealth Creation Principles

Below are some Wealth Creation Principles I am proposing for those who are serious about changing their financial status from poverty to wealth. It will also be beneficial to those who are already financially stable or wealthy but want to review how they acquire their wealth. Simply, the principles below can benefit the poor and the financially stable:

- Dig yourself out of debt slowly but methodically

- Keep wealth and power scriptures before your eyes

- Memorize scriptures that speaks of acquiring wealth

- Move from knowledge to action

- Be a giver; don't only seek to receive

- Change your mind-set from always wanting things for free. Abram paid for the tomb to bury his wife even though he could have gotten it free from the owner. (Genesis 23:17 – 20)

- Worship God ahead of time for the things you are believing Him for.

- Speak in faith over your financial situation and don't allow doubt to reside in your mind

- Do an audit of all your skills and abilities to assess your competence and areas mastery. These will become your servants to create multiple streams of

income as this is necessary for creating generational

wealth.

> Know your worth and the value of your time so that

when you decide to do something, you know the

value of your time vs opportunity. Knowing this

will result in better use of your time and you will

also realize that an opportunity for others is not

necessarily an opportunity for you.

Therefore, I thought it necessary to exhort the brethren to go to you ahead of time, and prepare your generous gift beforehand, which you had previously promised, that it may be ready as a matter of generosity

and not as a grudging obligation. But this I say: He who sows sparingly will also reap sparingly, and he who sows bountifully will also reap bountifully. So let each one give as he purposes in his heart, not grudgingly or of necessity; for God loves a cheerful giver. And God is able to make all grace abound toward you, that you, always having all sufficiency in all things, may have an abundance for every good work. (2 Corinthians 9: 5-8)

Another part of my transformation occurred one Sunday while worshipping in Church. I was standing and in worship when I felt this simple message in my spirit. The message was simple, *"Be a giver."* I wondered why the message was not *"Be a tither"* instead. I know that this is a controversial message, but I will try to make it brief. I know many Christians will disagree with me, but that is okay.

I'm just sharing my testimony, to encourage or inspire you, not to convince you. My new understanding is that God wants us to give, and scripture is clear that it is more blessed to give than to receive (Acts 20:35). How many persons have you seen give their tithe with a spirit of sadness, frustration and the fear of being cursed with a curse? I think giving is a happier place because you determine how much you want to give. Of course, the caveat is shown in 2 Corinthians 9:6-7, *"But this I say: He who sows sparingly will also reap sparingly, and he who sows bountifully will also reap bountifully. So let each one give as he purposes in his heart, not grudgingly or of necessity; for God loves a cheerful giver."*

It is my opinion that giving is a New Testament concept, while tithing is an Old Testament one. My understanding is that you cannot benefit from the Earth without contributing to it. You cannot be a part of a community without contributing to it, and the more you give, the more people respect you. I'm not proposing giving as an avenue to get respect from people, but I'm stating that you cannot expect to acquire and keep wealth without giving to others and the kingdom of God. In the New Testament, those who accepted Jesus Christ and were wealthy, sold some of their wealth and shared it with those who didn't have it. Acts 2: 44–46 (BSB) underscores this, *"All the believers were together and had everything in common. Selling their possessions and goods, they shared with anyone who was in need. With one accord, they continued to meet daily in the temple courts and to break bread from house to house, sharing their meals with gladness and sincerity of heart."* So you see, when you are in fellowship with God, you become a giver and, more importantly, a cheerful giver.

It's important to note that we should be honest in our hearts and listen to the Holy Spirit about giving. He may even tell us to give more than the usual amount on different occasions. If He does, it is so essential to be obedient as He knows the plans he has for us. He may want to open a substantial financial door for you. Don't operate under pretence because that is deception. If you cannot give what others expect of you, be sure to be honest, and say that you have changed your mind about the amount. Remember the story of Ananias and Sapphira? They didn't die because of the amount they gave; they died because they lied to the Holy Spirit about what they gave.

"But a certain man named Ananias, with Sapphira his wife, sold a possession, And kept back part of

the price, his wife also being privy to it, and brought a certain part, and laid it at the apostles' feet. But Peter said, Ananias, why hath Satan filled thine heart to lie to the Holy Ghost, and to keep back part of the price of the land? Whiles it remained, was it not thine own? And after it was sold, was it not in thine own power? why hast thou conceived this thing in thine heart? Thou hast not lied unto men, but unto God. And Ananias hearing these words fell down, and gave up the ghost: and great fear came on all them that heard these things. And the young men arose, wound him up, and carried him out, and buried him. And it was about the space of three hours after, when his wife, not knowing what was done, came in. And Peter answered unto her, Tell me whether ye sold the land for so much? And she said, Yea, for so much.

Then Peter said unto her, How is it that ye have agreed together to tempt the Spirit of the Lord? Behold, the feet of them which have buried thy husband are at the door, and shall carry thee out. Then fell she down straightway at his feet, and yielded up the ghost: and the young men came in, and found her dead, and, carrying her forth, buried her by her husband. And great fear came upon all the church, and upon as many as heard these things." (Acts 5:1-11)

Conclusion

It is my hope that this book on The Power to Get Wealth with a focus on Biblical Wealth has triggered in you a thought process on your past, present and future relationship with money. Feel free to disagree with any of the concepts or ideas presented, but I urge you to not only disagree but to research the answers you need to help you move forward. In a way, this is a testimonial of my own experiences and my new way forward. Indeed, I have felt fear and failed many times, but once I began to renew my mind, everything started to change. My prayer for you is that you will experience all the wealth that God has for you before you were conceived in your mother's womb and that whatever your life's challenges, you may encounter financial victory. May this information chart the way for

you testify to others about the power you received from

heaven.

God bless you and your household, and thank you

for taking the time to read The Power to Get Wealth.

References

https://bible.knowing-jesus.com/topics/God-Gives-Wealth

https://www.britannica.com/biography/Nefertiti

http://jamaica-gleaner.com/article/lead-stories/20160810/

cash-plus-payout-not-investors

www.ingramcontent.com/pod-product-compliance
Lightning Source LLC
Chambersburg PA
CBHW061259140726
47998CB00006B/2277